This notebook belongs to:

_____

_____

Date _____

Today I'm thankful for...!

_____
_____
_____
_____
_____
_____

The best moment of the day was...

_____
_____
_____
_____
_____

Rating

○ ○ ○ ○ ○

Thoughts and things to remember

_____

_____

_____

_____

_____

_____

_____

_____

_____

_____

_____

_____

_____

_____

_____

I wish

_____

_____

_____

_____

_____

_____

<u>Date</u>

Today I'm thankful for...!

_____
_____
_____
_____
_____
_____
_____
_____

The best moment of the day was...

_____
_____
_____
_____
_____
_____
_____

Rating

○ ○ ○ ○ ○

Thoughts and things to remember

I wish

Date

Today I'm thankful for...!

_____
_____
_____
_____
_____
_____
_____
_____

The best moment of the day was...

_____
_____
_____
_____
_____
_____
_____

Rating

Thoughts and things to remember

I wish

Date

Today I'm thankful for...!

The best moment of the day was...

Rating

Thoughts and things to remember

I wish

Date _____

Today I'm thankful for...!

_____
_____
_____
_____
_____
_____

The best moment of the day was...

_____
_____
_____
_____
_____
_____

Rating

Thoughts and things to remember

I wish

Date

Today I'm thankful for...!

The best moment of the day was...

Rating

Thoughts and things to remember

I wish

Date

Today I'm thankful for...!

_____
_____
_____
_____
_____
_____

The best moment of the day was...

_____
_____
_____
_____
_____
_____

Rating

○ ○ ○ ○ ○

Thoughts and things to remember

I wish

Date _____

Today I'm thankful for...!

_____
_____
_____
_____
_____
_____
_____

The best moment of the day was...

_____
_____
_____
_____
_____
_____

Rating

Thoughts and things to remember

I wish

Date

Today I'm thankful for...!

_____

_____

_____

_____

_____

_____

_____

The best moment of the day was...

_____

_____

_____

_____

_____

_____

Rating

Thoughts and things to remember

I wish

Date

Today I'm thankful for...!

_____
_____
_____
_____
_____
_____

The best moment of the day was...

_____
_____
_____
_____
_____

Rating

○ ○ ○ ○ ○

Thoughts and things to remember

_____

_____

_____

_____

_____

_____

_____

_____

_____

_____

_____

_____

_____

_____

_____

I wish

_____

_____

_____

_____

_____

_____

Date

Today I'm thankful for...!

_____
_____
_____
_____
_____
_____
_____
_____
_____

The best moment of the day was...

_____
_____
_____
_____
_____
_____
_____
_____

Rating

Thoughts and things to remember

I wish

Date

Today I'm thankful for...!

_____

_____

_____

_____

_____

_____

The best moment of the day was...

_____

_____

_____

_____

_____

_____

_____

Rating

Thoughts and things to remember

I wish

Date

Today I'm thankful for...!

_____
_____
_____
_____
_____
_____
_____

The best moment of the day was...

_____
_____
_____
_____
_____
_____

Rating

○ ○ ○ ○ ○

Thoughts and things to remember

I wish

Date

Today I'm thankful for...!

_____
_____
_____
_____
_____

The best moment of the day was...

_____
_____
_____
_____
_____

Rating

Thoughts and things to remember

I wish

Date

Today I'm thankful for...!

_____

_____

_____

_____

_____

_____

_____

The best moment of the day was...

_____

_____

_____

_____

_____

_____

Rating

Thoughts and things to remember

I wish

Date

Today I'm thankful for...!

_____
_____
_____
_____
_____
_____

The best moment of the day was...

_____
_____
_____
_____
_____

Rating

Thoughts and things to remember

I wish

Date

Today I'm thankful for...!

_____
_____
_____
_____
_____
_____
_____
_____

The best moment of the day was...

_____
_____
_____
_____
_____
_____
_____

Rating

Thoughts and things to remember

I wish

Date

Today I'm thankful for...!

_____
_____
_____
_____
_____
_____
_____

The best moment of the day was...

_____
_____
_____
_____
_____
_____

Rating

Thoughts and things to remember

I wish

Date

Today I'm thankful for...!

The best moment of the day was...

Rating

Thoughts and things to remember

I wish

Date

Today I'm thankful for...!

_____

_____

_____

_____

_____

The best moment of the day was...

_____

_____

_____

_____

_____

Rating

Thoughts and things to remember

I wish

Date

Today I'm thankful for...!

_____
_____
_____
_____
_____
_____

The best moment of the day was...

_____
_____
_____
_____
_____
_____

Rating

○ ○ ○ ○ ○

Thoughts and things to remember

I wish

Date _____

Today I'm thankful for...!

_____
_____
_____
_____
_____
_____

The best moment of the day was...

_____
_____
_____
_____
_____
_____

Rating

Thoughts and things to remember

I wish

Date

Today I'm thankful for...!

_____
_____
_____
_____
_____

The best moment of the day was...

_____
_____
_____
_____
_____
_____

Rating

Thoughts and things to remember

I wish

Date

Today I'm thankful for...!

The best moment of the day was...

Rating

Thoughts and things to remember

I wish

Date

Today I'm thankful for..!

_____
_____
_____
_____
_____
_____

The best moment of the day was...

_____
_____
_____
_____
_____
_____

Rating

○ ○ ○ ○ ○

Thoughts and things to remember

I wish

Date

Today I'm thankful for...!

The best moment of the day was...

Rating

Thoughts and things to remember

I wish

Date

Today I'm thankful for...!

The best moment of the day was...

Rating

Thoughts and things to remember

I wish

Date

Today I'm thankful for...!

The best moment of the day was...

Rating

Thoughts and things to remember

I wish

Date

Today I'm thankful for...!

_____
_____
_____
_____
_____
_____

The best moment of the day was...

_____
_____
_____
_____
_____
_____

Rating

○   ○   ○   ○   ○

Thoughts and things to remember

I wish

Date

Today I'm thankful for...!

_____
_____
_____
_____
_____
_____
_____
_____

The best moment of the day was...

_____
_____
_____
_____
_____
_____
_____

Rating

Thoughts and things to remember

I wish

Date

Today I'm thankful for...!

The best moment of the day was...

Rating

Thoughts and things to remember

I wish

Date

Today I'm thankful for...!

_____
_____
_____
_____
_____
_____

The best moment of the day was...

_____
_____
_____
_____
_____

Rating

Thoughts and things to remember

I wish

Date _____

Today I'm thankful for...!

_____
_____
_____
_____
_____
_____

The best moment of the day was...

_____
_____
_____
_____
_____
_____

Rating

Thoughts and things to remember

I wish

Date

Today I'm thankful for...!

The best moment of the day was...

Rating

Thoughts and things to remember

I wish

Date _____

Today I'm thankful for...!

_____
_____
_____
_____
_____
_____

The best moment of the day was...

_____
_____
_____
_____
_____
_____

Rating

Thoughts and things to remember

I wish

Date _____

Today I'm thankful for...!

_____
_____
_____
_____
_____
_____
_____

The best moment of the day was...

_____
_____
_____
_____
_____

Rating

Thoughts and things to remember

I wish

Date

Today I'm thankful for...!

_____
_____
_____
_____
_____
_____

The best moment of the day was...

_____
_____
_____
_____
_____
_____

Rating

Thoughts and things to remember

I wish

Date

Today I'm thankful for...!

_____

_____

_____

_____

_____

_____

The best moment of the day was...

_____

_____

_____

_____

_____

_____

Rating

○ ○ ○ ○ ○

Thoughts and things to remember

I wish

Date

Today I'm thankful for...!

_____
_____
_____
_____
_____
_____
_____

The best moment of the day was...

_____
_____
_____
_____
_____
_____

Rating

Thoughts and things to remember

I wish

Date

Today I'm thankful for...!

The best moment of the day was...

Rating

Thoughts and things to remember

I wish

Date _____

Today I'm thankful for...!

_____
_____
_____
_____
_____
_____

The best moment of the day was...

_____
_____
_____
_____
_____
_____

Rating

Thoughts and things to remember

I wish

Date

Today I'm thankful for...!

_____

_____

_____

_____

_____

_____

_____

The best moment of the day was...

_____

_____

_____

_____

_____

_____

Rating

Thoughts and things to remember

I wish

Date _____

Today I'm thankful for...!

_____
_____
_____
_____
_____
_____
_____
_____

The best moment of the day was...

_____
_____
_____
_____
_____
_____
_____

Rating

○ ○ ○ ○ ○

Thoughts and things to remember

I wish

Date _____

Today I'm thankful for...!

_____
_____
_____
_____
_____
_____
_____

The best moment of the day was...

_____
_____
_____
_____
_____
_____

Rating

Thoughts and things to remember

I wish

Date _____

Today I'm thankful for...!

_____
_____
_____
_____
_____
_____
_____

The best moment of the day was...

_____
_____
_____
_____
_____
_____
_____

Rating

Thoughts and things to remember

I wish

Date

Today I'm thankful for...!

_____
_____
_____
_____
_____
_____
_____
_____

The best moment of the day was...

_____
_____
_____
_____
_____
_____

Rating

Thoughts and things to remember

I wish

Date _____

Today I'm thankful for...!

_____
_____
_____
_____
_____
_____
_____

The best moment of the day was...

_____
_____
_____
_____
_____
_____

Rating

Thoughts and things to remember

I wish

Date

Today I'm thankful for...!

The best moment of the day was...

Rating

Thoughts and things to remember

I wish

Date

Today I'm thankful for...!

The best moment of the day was...

Rating

Thoughts and things to remember

I wish

Date _____

Today I'm thankful for...!

_____
_____
_____
_____
_____
_____
_____
_____
_____

The best moment of the day was...

_____
_____
_____
_____
_____
_____
_____
_____

Rating

Thoughts and things to remember

I wish

Date _____

Today I'm thankful for...!

_____
_____
_____
_____
_____
_____

The best moment of the day was...

_____
_____
_____
_____
_____
_____

Rating

Thoughts and things to remember

I wish

Date

Today I'm thankful for...!

_____
_____
_____
_____
_____
_____
_____

The best moment of the day was...

_____
_____
_____
_____
_____
_____

Rating

○ ○ ○ ○ ○

Thoughts and things to remember

I wish

Date _____

Today I'm thankful for...!

_____
_____
_____
_____
_____
_____
_____
_____
_____

The best moment of the day was...

_____
_____
_____
_____
_____
_____
_____
_____

Rating

Thoughts and things to remember

I wish

Date _____

Today I'm thankful for...!

_____
_____
_____
_____
_____
_____

The best moment of the day was...

_____
_____
_____
_____
_____

Rating

Thoughts and things to remember

I wish